W9-CUI-075

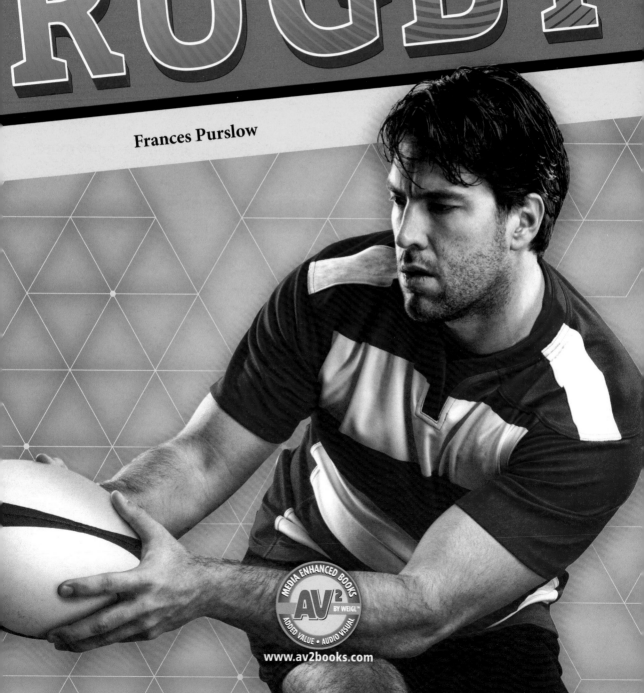

FOR THE LOVE OF SPORTS

RUGBY

Frances Purslow

AV² provides enriched content that supplements and complements this book. Weigl's AV² books strive to create inspired learning and engage young minds in a total learning experience.

Your AV² Media Enhanced books come alive with...

Audio
Listen to sections of the book read aloud.

Key Words
Study vocabulary, and complete a matching word activity.

Go to www.av2books.com, and enter this book's unique code.

Video
Watch informative video clips.

Quizzes
Test your knowledge.

BOOK CODE

AVE72629

Embedded Weblinks
Gain additional information for research.

Slide Show
View images and captions, and prepare a presentation.

AV² by Weigl brings you media enhanced books that support active learning.

Try This!
Complete activities and hands-on experiments.

... and much, much more!

Published by AV² by Weigl
350 5th Avenue, 59th Floor
New York, NY 10118
Website: www.av2books.com

Library of Congress Control Number: 2018965256

ISBN 978-1-7911-0017-9 (hardcover)
ISBN 978-1-7911-0572-3 (softcover)
ISBN 978-1-7911-0018-6 (multi-user eBook)
ISBN 978-1-7911-0019-3 (single-user eBook)

Printed in the United States of America in Brainerd, Minnesota
1 2 3 4 5 6 7 8 9 0 22 21 20 19 18

122018
103118

Project Coordinator: John Willis
Art Director: Terry Paulhus

Photo Credits
Every reasonable effort has been made to trace ownership and to obtain permission to reprint copyright material. The publishers would be pleased to have any errors or omissions brought to their attention so that they may be corrected in subsequent printings.

Weigl acknowledges Alamy and Getty Images as its primary image suppliers for this title.

FOR THE LOVE OF SPORTS
RUGBY

CONTENTS

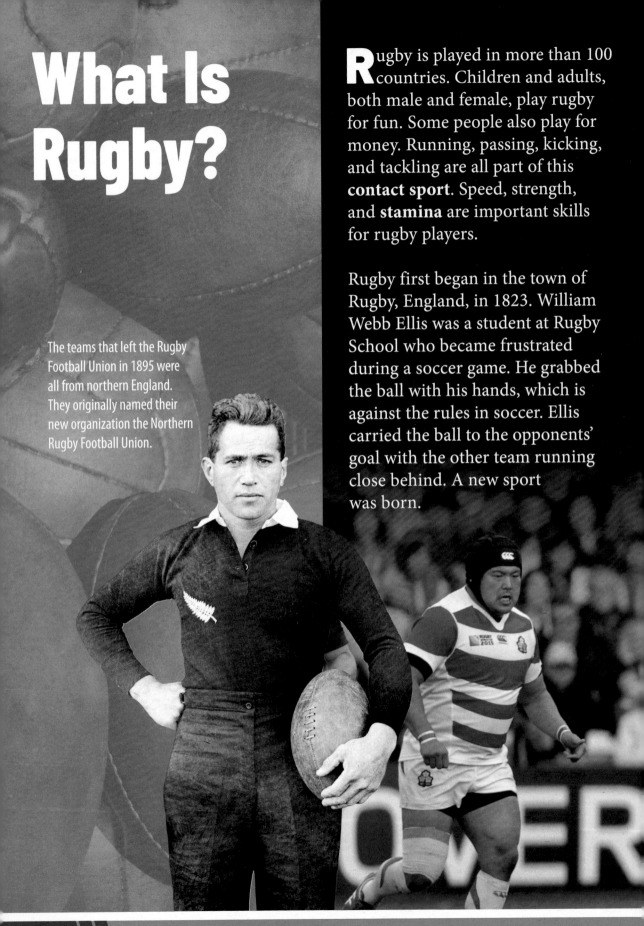

What Is Rugby?

Rugby is played in more than 100 countries. Children and adults, both male and female, play rugby for fun. Some people also play for money. Running, passing, kicking, and tackling are all part of this **contact sport**. Speed, strength, and **stamina** are important skills for rugby players.

Rugby first began in the town of Rugby, England, in 1823. William Webb Ellis was a student at Rugby School who became frustrated during a soccer game. He grabbed the ball with his hands, which is against the rules in soccer. Ellis carried the ball to the opponents' goal with the other team running close behind. A new sport was born.

The teams that left the Rugby Football Union in 1895 were all from northern England. They originally named their new organization the Northern Rugby Football Union.

Students continued to play rugby football. The game spread to other schools. In 1839, a team was established at the University of Cambridge in England. A set of rules for rugby was created at the same time. In 1871, a number of rugby teams came together in London to form the Rugby Football Union. Later that year, the first **international** rugby game was played between England and Scotland.

In rugby union, players lift each other to try and catch the ball when it is thrown back into play after going out of bounds. This is called a lineout.

Some of the clubs in the Rugby Football Union disagreed on whether players should be paid for playing rugby. In 1895, 22 clubs left the Rugby Football Union and eventually created a slightly different sport, called "rugby league." The sport of the Rugby Football Union came to be known as "rugby union," or just "rugby." Each sport has its own code, or set of rules. One of the big differences is the number of players on the field. Each team in a rugby league game has two fewer players. World Rugby, previously known as the International Rugby Board (IRB), uses the code of rugby union. These rules are used in more countries around the world than the rules of rugby league, including the United States and Canada.

There are more than **900** college rugby teams in the United States.

With **20,000** registered players, the United States has more female rugby players than any other country.

USA Rugby has more than **3,700 referees**.

Getting Ready to Play

The first rugby balls were made of hand-stitched leather. Today, most have rubber on the outer surface.

Rugby teams wear uniforms when they play. Players do not need a lot of equipment to play rugby. The most important piece of equipment needed to play rugby is a rugby ball.

A rugby ball is oval and made of four panels. It is slightly rounder and larger than a football. The rugby ball is 11 to 12 inches (28 to 30 centimeters) long and 23 to 24 inches (58 to 62 cm) around the middle. The ball weighs between 14 and 16 ounces (410 and 460 grams).

Rugby jerseys have the team logo on the chest and the logo of team sponsors in other places on the uniform.

Players wear a mouth guard to protect their teeth and help prevent head injuries.

Rugby players wear jerseys with their number on the back. Jerseys are made of tough material so they do not rip easily. Some players also wear light shoulder padding under their uniforms.

Some players wear special caps to protect their ears. Other players wrap tape around their head to hold their ears flat instead.

Players wear shorts and long socks that match the colors of their team.

The Pitch

Rugby is played on a grass field called a pitch. It is a bit longer and wider than a football field. The pitches for both rugby union and rugby league are 109 yards (100 meters) long. Rugby union fields are 2 yards (2.5 m) wider than rugby league fields.

There is a try zone at each end of the field. The try zone is sometimes called the in-goal area. White lines mark the boundaries of the pitch. Goalposts are set on the goal line at either end of the pitch. The goalposts are shaped like the letter "H." The posts are 18 feet (5.5 m) apart. There is a crossbar connecting them 10 feet (3 m) above the ground. The goalposts are usually covered with padding, so players will not be hurt if they run into them.

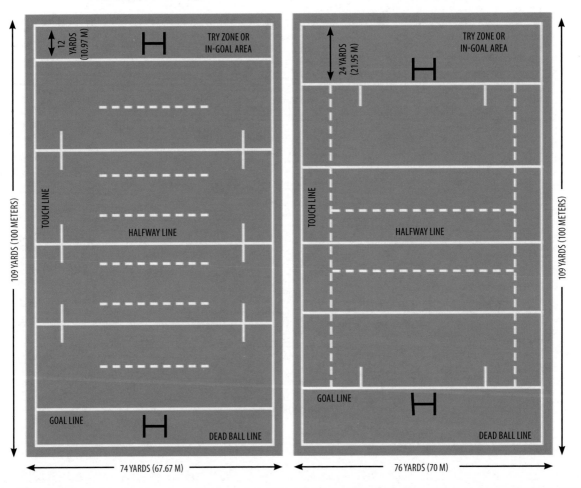

RUGBY LEAGUE

12 YARDS (10.97 M)

TRY ZONE OR IN-GOAL AREA

TOUCH LINE

HALFWAY LINE

109 YARDS (100 METERS)

GOAL LINE

DEAD BALL LINE

74 YARDS (67.67 M)

RUGBY UNION

24 YARDS (21.95 M)

TRY ZONE OR IN-GOAL AREA

TOUCH LINE

HALFWAY LINE

109 YARDS (100 METERS)

GOAL LINE

DEAD BALL LINE

76 YARDS (70 M)

Tournaments

World Rugby has competitions all over the world for both men's and women's teams. Depending on the season, there are between four and six tournaments. Past years have seen events played in England, France, Japan, Australia, and the United States.

The opening round of the HSBC World Rugby Women's Sevens Series was played in Glendale, Colorado, in 2018. It is the first major tournament that begins the World Rugby Women's Sevens Series. In this event, different countries compete in various tournaments to be the best.

Rugby Basics

A rugby game is called a match. One referee and two judges oversee the match. It is played in two 40-minute halves with a 5-to-10-minute break at halftime. The teams switch ends after halftime.

A rugby ball cannot be passed forward. Players can carry it forward or kick it forward, but they can only pass it to teammates beside or behind them. The team with the most points after 80 minutes wins the match.

There are many ways to score points in rugby. Teams get the most points for scoring a try. This happens when the ball carrier runs across the goal line and touches the ball on the ground. A try is worth five points in rugby union and four points in rugby league.

A penalty kick is worth three points in Rugby Union and two points in Rugby League.

After a try is scored, a player on the team kicks the ball to gain more points for his or her team. Kickers can **place kick** or **drop kick** the ball as far out from the goal line as they want, but it must line up with where the ball was touched down in the try zone. If the ball goes through the goalposts, the team gains two points.

At any time, any player can try to drop kick the ball through the goalposts. This means that for any of these kicks to be successful, they must pass between the goalposts and above the crossbar. The final way to score points is with a **penalty kick**. Referees can call penalties for many different **infractions**. When a team is awarded a penalty, the team captain can choose to kick for the goal or run with the ball.

If play is stopped due to an infraction, the forwards take part in a **scrum** to get the ball back in play. They link together by putting their arms around each other's shoulders. Then, they bend at the waist. At a signal from the referee, they engage, or **interlock**, with the forwards of the other team. Each group tries to overpower the other with its strength. The ball is rolled into the opening between the feet of the two groups. Each team tries to use their feet to hook the ball to a teammate outside of the scrum.

The scrum-half rolls the ball into the scrum.

Positions

In rugby union, each team has 15 players on the field. There are eight forwards and seven backs. In rugby league, each team has two fewer players on the field. There are six forwards and seven backs in rugby league.

The number on a player's jersey is determined by the position he or she plays on the field. In rugby union, forwards wear numbers 1 to 8 and backs wear numbers 9 to 15. In rugby league, the forwards wear numbers 8 to 13 and backs wear numbers 1 to 7.

Forwards are big, strong players that form the scrum. Three forwards are in the front row of the scrum. The middle forward is the hooker. It is the hooker's job to kick the ball back to his or her teammates.

The second row of forwards in the scrum supports the first row. They try to overpower the other team and get possession of the ball. When the ball rolls out of the scrum, the forwards pass the ball to the backs.

Rugby uniforms usually have numbers only on the back of the shirt, not on the font.

The scrum-half plays right behind the forwards. This player is the link between the forwards and the backs. It is similar to being the quarterback in football. When the ball comes out of the scrum, the scrum-half decides which back is in the best position to receive the ball.

The backs then run the ball up the field. They can pass the ball to other backs who are running beside them or behind them. If a back is tackled to the ground by the other team, they must drop the ball. Players from each team surround the ball and form a ruck. A ruck is similar to a scrum. Players in a ruck try to push the other team backward so their backs can get the ball.

If a player with the ball is stopped but is not tackled to the ground, a maul is formed. Each team surrounds the ball carrier and tries to gain possession of the ball using their arms and hands.

The two forwards beside the hooker are called props. They help get the hooker in position to kick the ball back to their team.

BACKS

Most rugby passes are thrown underhand.

Running with two hands on the ball makes it easier for the player to either pass or kick the ball before being tackled.

PROPS

Where the Action Is

Many boys and girls play rugby on community teams. Some of the leagues for younger players are non-contact. When players are older, they can play on high school, college, and university teams. They can also play for club teams. In North America, leagues have games and tournaments that are **endorsed** by USA Rugby and Rugby Canada.

Many cities in England have **professional** teams. Some cities in North America have professional teams as well. Professional players who play for these teams have the chance to be selected to play for their country's national team.

In non-contact leagues, players wear flags or are touched instead of being tackled.

When a rugby player plays for his or her country in an international match, it is called a cap.

The three key international rugby tournaments are the Rugby World Cup, Six Nations Championship, and the Rugby Championship.

The first Rugby World Cup was hosted by New Zealand and Australia in 1987. The tournament allows a country to establish itself as the world champion of rugby. The event takes place every four years. The U.S. national team is called the Eagles. The Eagles have played in seven of the eight Rugby World Cup competitions. The Women's Rugby World Cup also occurs every four years. It is held on different years than the men's event.

The countries involved in the Six Nations Championship are England, Ireland, Scotland, Wales, France, and Italy. The tournament is played every year. It started in 1883 between England, Ireland, Scotland, and Wales. France joined in 1910, and Italy joined in 2000.

The Rugby Championship used to be called Tri Nations. It started in 1996 as a tournament between Australia, New Zealand, and South Africa. The New Zealand All Blacks have won the tournament 16 times. The name was changed to the Rugby Championship when Argentina joined the event in 2012.

Twenty teams compete in the Rugby World Cup for the Webb Ellis Cup. The championship trophy is named after the boy who started the sport of rugby. New Zealand has won the Webb Ellis Cup three times.

After all the hard work during the game, the winning team can celebrate.

History of Rugby

Although Rugby has been around for nearly 150 years, it has been slow to gain a large fan base. Today, more and more men and women are beginning to play rugby around the world. The United States is becoming more competitive as the sport gains popularity.

The 1995 Rugby World Cup was held in Johannesburg, South Africa. South African president Nelson Mandela presented his country's team with the Webb Ellis Cup after South Africa won in the finals by a score of 15–12.

1874 The first recorded rugby match in the United States is played on May 14, 1874. However, unofficial games were played as early as the 1840s.

1912 The first international rugby match is played between University of California, Berkeley and Australia's national rugby team. Australia wins 12–8.

1920  The United States wins its first gold medal in Olympic rugby.

1975 USA Rugby is founded. This organization maintains rules and club teams all over the United States.

2016 The Summer Olympics holds a rugby tournament for the first time since 1924. Fiji wins the gold in men's rugby and Australia wins the gold in women's rugby.

2019 The ninth Rugby World Cup is held in Japan. This marks the first time the event has ever been held in Asia.

*Rugby is most popular in South Africa, where more than **340,000** people are registered as rugby players.*

*Most rugby players are between **22** and **29** years old.*

*Until 1870, the rugby ball was **round**. After 1870, the ball became **egg-shaped**.*

Superstars of Rugby

The sport of rugby has attracted many superb athletes. They thrill fans who fill the stands.

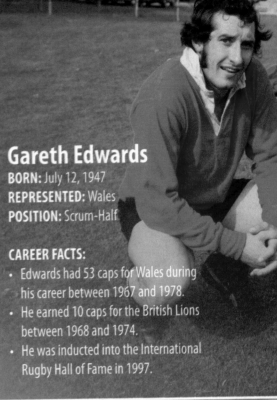

Gareth Edwards

BORN: July 12, 1947
REPRESENTED: Wales
POSITION: Scrum-Half

CAREER FACTS:

- Edwards had 53 caps for Wales during his career between 1967 and 1978.
- He earned 10 caps for the British Lions between 1968 and 1974.
- He was inducted into the International Rugby Hall of Fame in 1997.

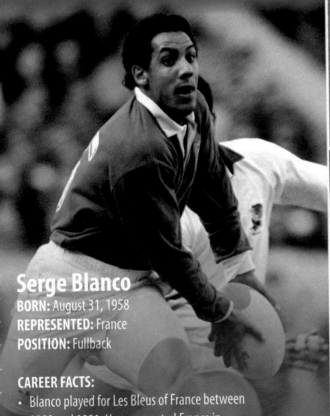

Serge Blanco

BORN: August 31, 1958
REPRESENTED: France
POSITION: Fullback

CAREER FACTS:

- Blanco played for Les Bleus of France between 1980 and 1991. He represented France in international matches 93 times during those years.
- He was inducted into the International Rugby Hall of Fame in 1997 and the World Rugby Hall of Fame in 2011.
- Blanco was often known as the "Superman of rugby." He scored 233 points for France during his career.

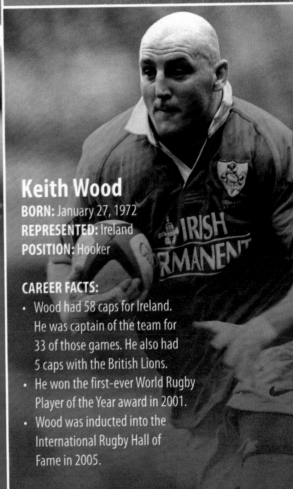

Keith Wood

BORN: January 27, 1972
REPRESENTED: Ireland
POSITION: Hooker

CAREER FACTS:

- Wood had 58 caps for Ireland. He was captain of the team for 33 of those games. He also had 5 caps with the British Lions.
- He won the first-ever World Rugby Player of the Year award in 2001.
- Wood was inducted into the International Rugby Hall of Fame in 2005.

John Eales

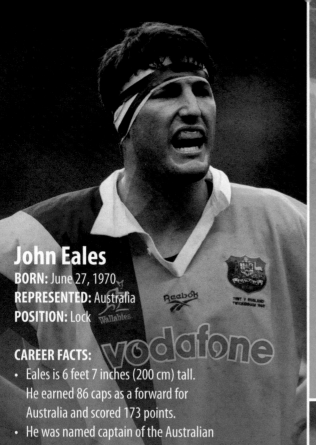

BORN: June 27, 1970
REPRESENTED: Australia
POSITION: Lock

CAREER FACTS:
- Eales is 6 feet 7 inches (200 cm) tall. He earned 86 caps as a forward for Australia and scored 173 points.
- He was named captain of the Australian team 55 times. His team won the World Cup in 1991 and 1999.
- Eales was inducted into the International Rugby Hall of Fame in 2005.

Jonny Wilkinson

BORN: May 25, 1979
REPRESENTED: England
POSITION: Fly-Half

CAREER FACTS:
- Wilkinson scored a drop goal in the final seconds of the 2003 World Cup final. England beat Australia 20–17. He won the World Rugby International Player of the Year award that year.
- He has scored 1,179 points for the England national team.
- He was the third player in history to win the Golden Boot award for reaching 1,000 points in England's premier league.

Bryan Habana

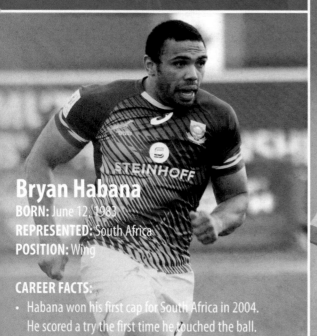

BORN: June 12, 1983
REPRESENTED: South Africa
POSITION: Wing

CAREER FACTS:
- Habana won his first cap for South Africa in 2004. He scored a try the first time he touched the ball.
- He became South Africa's all-time leader in tries during the 2011 World Cup.

Todd Clever

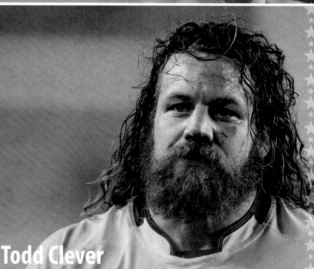

BORN: January 16, 1983
REPRESENTED: United States
POSITION: Flanker

CAREER FACTS:
- Clever earned his first cap for the United States in 2003 versus Argentina.
- He has played professional rugby in the United States, New Zealand, South Africa, and Japan.
- Clever has earned 74 caps for the U.S. national team. He has scored 16 tries and 80 points for the Eagles.

Staying Healthy

There is a great deal of running in rugby, so players have to keep their bodies in good shape. They need to eat healthy foods and drink plenty of water. Eating balanced meals helps athletes work harder for longer periods of time.

The night before a match, many athletes eat **carbohydrates**, such as pasta, bread, and rice. The body stores this type of food as energy in the muscles and helps keep players from getting tired during a match.

Foods from the other food groups, such as fruits, vegetables, protein, and milk products, also have important **nutrients** needed for a healthy body. Strong bones and muscles are important when playing a sport that requires speed and strength.

Athletes need to drink fluids before, during, and after exercising.

Fruits and vegetables provide vitamins and minerals to keep athletes healthy.

Athletes need to drink water to replace what they lose when they sweat. When muscles work hard, they produce heat in the body. To keep cool, the body releases heat through sweat.

Rugby teams do warm-up drills before matches to help prevent injury.

- 1 -

What did clubs in the **Rugby Football Union** disagree on?

- 2 -

When **22 teams** left the Rugby Football Union, what did they **create**?

- 3 -

What is the **biggest difference** between rugby league and rugby union games?

- 4 -

The **International Rugby Board** uses the rules from which type of rugby?

THE RUGBY QUIZ

- 5 -

How many rugby **referees** does USA Rugby have?

- 6 -

What is the **grass field** called where rugby is played?

- 7 -

What is a **rugby** game called?

- 8 -

How many **points** is a **try** worth in rugby union?

- 9 -

When was **USA Rugby** founded?

- 10 -

Who won the 2016 Olympic **gold medal** in men's rugby?

ANSWERS: 1 Whether players should be paid 2 Rugby league 3 The number of players on the field 4 Rugby Union 5 More than 3,700 6 A field 7 A match 8 Five points 9 1975 10 Fiji

Key Words

carbohydrates: foods that provide energy

contact sport: a sport where physical contact is allowed

drop kick: a kick when the ball is dropped from the player's hands

endorsed: supported

infractions: errors or broken rules

interlock: connect two or more things together

international: involving two or more countries

nutrients: substances needed by the body and obtained from food

penalty kick: a place kick that occurs after a penalty is called and the kicker thinks he is within range to score

place kick: a kick in which the ball is placed on a plastic tee on the ground

professional: an athlete who earns money for playing a sport

scrum: when the forwards on each team come together and try to gain possession of the ball

stamina: the ability to do something for a long time

Index

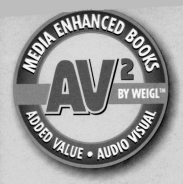

Log on to www.av2books.com

AV² by Weigl brings you media enhanced books that support active learning. Go to www.av2books.com, and enter the special code found on page 2 of this book. You will gain access to enriched and enhanced content that supplements and complements this book. Content includes video, audio, weblinks, quizzes, a slide show, and activities.

AV² Online Navigation

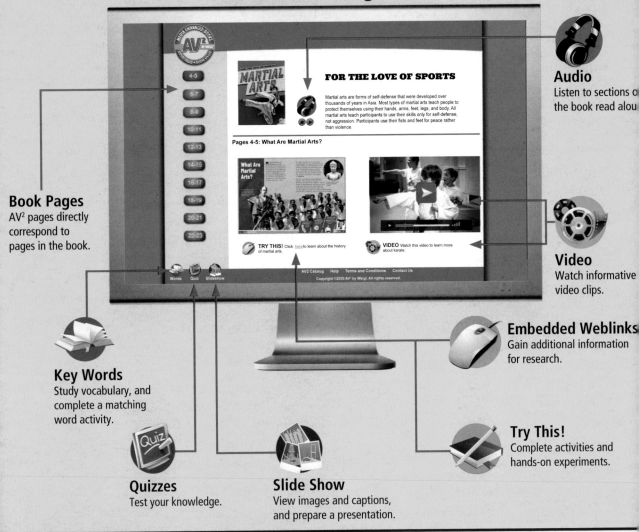

Audio
Listen to sections o
the book read alou

Book Pages
AV² pages directly correspond to pages in the book.

Video
Watch informative video clips.

Key Words
Study vocabulary, and complete a matching word activity.

Embedded Weblinks
Gain additional information for research.

Try This!
Complete activities and hands-on experiments.

Quizzes
Test your knowledge.

Slide Show
View images and captions, and prepare a presentation.

AV² was built to bridge the gap between print and digital. We encourage you to tell us what you like and what you want to see in the future.

Sign up to be an AV² Ambassador at www.av2books.com/ambassador.